hero

These quotations were gathered lovingly but unscientifically over several years and/or contributed by many friends or acquaintances. Some arrived, and survived in our files, on scraps of paper and may therefore be imperfectly worded or attributed. To the authors, contributors and original sources, our thanks, and where appropriate, our apologies.—The Editors

CREDITS

Compiled by Kobi Yamada
Designed by Steve Potter

ISBN: 978-1-888387-64-3

Printed in China

One by one, we can be
the better world we wish for.

KOBI YAMADA

Also available are these spirited companion books in The Good Life series of great quotations:

drive
friend
heart
hope
joy
moxie
refresh
service
spirit
success
thanks
value
vision
welcome
yes!

There is no more noble occupation in the world than to assist another human being— to help someone succeed.

ALAN LOY McGINNIS

THE GREAT LESSON IS THAT THE

SACRED IS IN THE ORDINARY, THAT

IT IS TO BE FOUND IN ONE'S DAILY

LIFE, IN ONE'S NEIGHBORS, FRIENDS,

AND FAMILY, IN ONE'S BACK YARD.

ABRAHAM MASLOW

If you
cannot feed
a hundred people,
then feed
just one.

MOTHER TERESA

EACH HEART HAS AN ENORMOUS
CAPACITY TO HOLD THE WORLD.

JACK KORNFIELD

I believe that one of the most important things to learn in life is that you can make a difference in your community no matter who you are or where you live. I have seen so many good deeds, people helped, lives improved, because someone cared...Do what you can to show you care about other people, and you will make our world a better place.

ROSALYNN CARTER

Every man is entitled

to be valued by

his best moments.

RALPH WALDO EMERSON

THROUGH REVERENCE

FOR LIFE I RAISE MY

EXISTENCE TO ITS

HIGHEST VALUE AND

OFFER IT TO THE WORLD.

ALBERT SCHWEITZER

Be sure you

put your feet

in the right

place, then

stand firm.

ABRAHAM LINCOLN

Efforts and courage
are not enough
without
purpose and
direction.

JOHN F. KENNEDY

For things to change,

we must change.

For things to get better,

we must get better.

HEIDI WILLS

WE VOTE WITH OUR ACTIONS.

BENJAMIN SHIELD

How far you go in life depends on your being tender with the young, compassionate with the aged, sympathetic with the striving, and tolerant of the weak and strong, because some-day in your life, you will have been all of these.

GEORGE WASHINGTON CARVER

So act that your principle of

action might safely be made

law for the whole world.

IMMANUEL KANT

A HUMAN
ACT ONCE SET IN
MOTION FLOWS ON
FOREVER TO
THE GREAT ACCOUNT.

GEORGE MEREDITH

If something comes to life in others

because of you, then you have

made an approach to immortality.

NORMAN COUSINS

Live so that
your children
can tell
their children
that you
not only stood
for something
wonderful—
you acted
on it.

DAN ZADRA

One must
care about
a world one
will not see.

BERTRAND RUSSELL

THE WELFARE OF EACH IS BOUND
UP IN THE WELFARE OF ALL.

H E L E N   K E L L E R

The world
will be saved
by one or two
people at a time.

ANDRE GIDE

There is not

enough darkness

in all the world

to put out the light

of even one

small candle.

ROBERT ALDEN

It is extraordinary how extraordinary the ordinary person is.

GEORGE F. WILL

Most people are like you and me, or the people across the street or around the world from you and me. Just like you and me, their hearts tell them that somewhere, somehow they can make a positive difference in the world.

WILLIAM BAKER

A hero is simply someone

who rises above his or her

own human weaknesses,

for an hour, a day, a year,

to do something stirring.

BETTY DERAMUS

We stand in
life at midnight,
we are always
on the threshold
of a new dawn.

MARTIN LUTHER KING, JR.

No soul that aspires can ever fail

to rise; no heart that loves can ever

be abandoned. Difficulties exist

only that in overcoming them we

may grow strong, and they who

have suffered are able to save.

ANNIE BESANT

Oh, my friend,
it's not
what they
take away
from you
that counts.
It's what you
do with what
you have left.

HUBERT HUMPHREY

To endure is greater than to dare; to tire out the hostile fortune; to be daunted by no difficulty; to keep heart when all have lost it—who can say this is not greatness?

WILLIAM MAKEPEACE THACKERAY

Strength has a million faces.

DES'REE

IF THE WORLD IS TO BE HEALED

THROUGH HUMAN EFFORTS,

I AM CONVINCED IT WILL BE

BY ORDINARY PEOPLE,

PEOPLE WHOSE LOVE FOR

THIS LIFE IS EVEN GREATER

THAN THEIR FEAR.

JOANNA MACY

It takes courage

for people to listen

to their own

goodness

and act on it.

PABLO CASALS

I am only one, but still
I am one. I cannot do
everything, but still
I can do something.
And because I cannot
do everything, I will
not refuse to do the
something that I can do.

HELEN KELLER

To be courageous requires no exceptional qualifications, no magic formula. It's an opportunity that sooner or later is presented to us all and each person must look for that courage in his own soul.

JOHN F. KENNEDY

WE NEVER
KNOW HOW HIGH
WE ARE
TILL WE ARE
ASKED TO RISE
AND THEN IF
WE ARE TRUE TO PLAN
OUR STATURES
TOUCH THE SKIES.

EMILY DICKINSON

It is not only

for what we do

that we are held

responsible, but

also for what

we do not do.

MOLIÈRE

YOU MUST
NEVER BE FEARFUL
ABOUT WHAT YOU ARE DOING
WHEN IT IS
RIGHT.

ROSA PARKS

When we do face
the difficult times,
we need to remember
that circumstances
don't make a person,
they reveal a person.

EMMA JAMESON

We must have a pure, honest and

warm-hearted motivation, and on top

of that, determination, optimism,

hope, and the ability not to be

discouraged. The whole of humanity

depends on this motivation.

THE DALAI LAMA

WE CAN CHOOSE

TO BE AFFECTED

BY THE WORLD OR

WE CAN CHOOSE TO

AFFECT THE WORLD.

HEIDI WILLS

I think the
purpose of life
is to be useful,
responsible,
honorable,
compassionate.
It is, above all,
to matter: to count,
to stand for
something, to have
made some
difference that
you lived at all.

LEO ROSTEN

In the morning ask yourself, "What good shall I do today?" As the day draws to a close ask yourself, "What good have I done today?"

BENJAMIN FRANKLIN

We are here to add

what we can to,

not to get what we

can from, life.

SIR WILLIAM OSLER

The future belongs to those who believe in the beauty of their dreams. In the long run, we shape our lives, and we shape our-selves. The process never ends until we die.

ELEANOR ROOSEVELT

IT TAKES EACH OF US
TO MAKE A DIFFERENCE FOR ALL OF US.

JACKIE MUTCHESON

This I know. This I believe with all my heart. If we want a free and peaceful world, if we want to make deserts bloom and man to grow to greater dignity as a human being—we can do it!

ELEANOR ROOSEVELT

We have enough people who tell it like it is—now we could use a few who tell it like it can be.

ROBERT ORBEN

TO THE WORLD
YOU MAY BE
JUST ONE
PERSON,
BUT TO ONE PERSON
YOU MAY BE THE
WORLD.

JOSEPHINE BILLINGS

Everyone who does the best he or she can do should be considered a hero.

JOSH BILLINGS

All this will not be

finished in the first

100 days. Nor will

it be finished in the

first 1000 days.

Nor even perhaps

in our lifetime

on this planet.

But let us begin.

JOHN F. KENNEDY

Someone is enjoying

shade today because

someone planted a tree

a long time ago.

WARREN   BUFFETT

We can live
a life full and
complete,
thinking with
our heads
but living from
our hearts.

HELEN HUNT, M.A.

WHAT WE DO
TODAY,
RIGHT NOW, WILL HAVE AN
ACCUMULATED
EFFECT ON
ALL OUR TOMORROWS.

ALEXANDRA STODDARD

There are those whose lives affect all others around them. Quietly touching one heart, who in turn, touches another. Reaching out to ends further than they would ever know.

WILLIAM BRADFIELD

SOME PEOPLE

STRENGTHEN OUR SOCIETY

JUST BY BEING

THE KIND OF PEOPLE

THEY ARE.

JOHN W. GARDNER

Act as if

what you do

makes a difference.

It does.

WILLIAM JAMES

Nurture your minds with great thoughts. To believe in the heroic makes heroes.

BENJAMIN DISRAELI

The world knows little
about its greatest heroes.

D A N   Z A D R A